The Fairy Luna
By Anne Swartz

This book is dedicated to
Jay Lose and Charles Lose

Copyright © 2023

All Rights Reserved. No part of this book may be reproduced or used in any manner without written permission of the copyright owner except for the use of quotations in a book review.

ISBN: 979-8-9876520-2-2 (Paperback)
ISBN: 979-8-9876520-3-9 (eBook)

Published by Aram Samsam Printing

Other titles by Anne Swartz
Nobody Likes Eddie, illustrated by Fred Dasinger
Who Wears A Beard?
Milekah Speech Therapist

Once upon a time, fairies and witches lived together relatively peacefully in the Land of the Mythical Forest.

Both of them were powerful.

Fairies might look young and beautiful or swift and fierce. They had a delicate sweetness and a feathery lightness.

They tended to want beauty and happiness. They liked to dance with flowers and butterflies. They wore many colors.

The witches could control their appearance, age, and energy. They could seem graceful and calm, then old and weak in a matter of moments.

They were powerful, tricky, and wild. They loved to dance in fields, sometimes all night long. They usually wore all black.

The pair were in continuous communication, but their lives were challenging. Sometimes angry witches moved from one land to another. They made the energy for fairies and witches not work sometimes and life difficult for them to live together easily.

One of those angry witches was Rozsika. She visited their land and cast an awful spell.

Luna, a young fairy full of kindness and adventure, lived in this enchanted land. She possessed extraordinary abilities and wore dresses made of flowers.

Luna would change her appearance depending on her mood. She might look a little older or younger, milder or more intense.

Luna knew the answers to the other fairies' questions before they even asked them. She was an expert on animals and plants and often knew how to change things no one else could understand.

She would help everyone, even the farmers who sometimes needed their cows to fly or wanted them to stop flying.

While on an adventure one day, the sweet fairy Luna came upon a weeping clan of fairies she had not seen recently. Each one Luna knew as a happy person, joyful, singing, and dancing all day long.

But on this day, they were crying together. They called and cried with tears like little jewels rolling down their faces.

The sad fairies told Luna their woodlands had been trapped under a spell imposed by Rozsika, the scary witch, making all the trees, plants, and animals sad and sickly.

Rozsika had cast the mad spell out of anger when all the witches and fairies in the Land of the Mythical Forest refused to serve her every whim.

The crying fairies told Luna, "Our witches had controlled the scary witch, offering her entertainment by making the forest more beautiful than before."

The very sad fairies continued, "Each day, the witches would invent some new wonderful way to make Rozsika see the world as more beautiful."

But Rozsika could not be satisfied. She wanted more excitement, and no one could move rapidly enough to organize enough festivities in her honor.

The fairies said sadly, "In anger, Rozsika cast a curse over our valley that we have not been able to remove."

The worried fairies wailed, "The local friendly witches' charms protected us at the start. Now, their special potions are losing power. Nature is failing. We need help. Can you help us, Luna?"

Luna yelled, "Oh no! Everything about this is awful. How do we put a stop to this?"

She could see the fairies' radiance flickering chaotically from frustration. This situation made her angry.

Luna realized she needed to use her determination and strength to organize the fairies and help them.

She proclaimed, "I refuse to give up. Let's find your local friendly witches and get their help. Together, we can destroy the wicked witch's enchantments."

She had set her mind on victory. The fairies were excited.

Luna wanted to protect the forest. She rounded up her fairy pals and set off to track down the good local witches and end Rozsika's awful curse.

Luna encouraged the fairies to feel confident all working together. There were many of them, and she knew there was strength in numbers.

She encouraged the fairies to believe in themselves and their powers.

The fairies lived deep in the forest. To travel to the good local witches, there were snarling branches to avoid and tall trees to soar over as the fairies made their way through the woods.

The fairies traveled toward the castle where the friendly local witches lived. It was a large gray stone structure with many pointing edges.

The friendly witches knew they were coming and waited to look out for them. The trees had whispered about the fairies coming to the witches. The trees had spoken to them and told them the fairies were on their way to ask for help.

The friendly witches were ready and waiting for them but did not know what to say to them because they could not stop Rozsika's curse.

When they met, taking the initiative, Luna put on a brave face and boldly proclaimed, "We need your help to break Rozsika's evil spell left on this woodland. We need your help now!"

There were several witches. One raised her hands, telling Luna to stop. She said, "Do you seriously believe we can dispel that scary witch's magic? It's far too potent."

Luna knew that together the powers of the witches and the fairies could conquer much and restore the beauty of the forest.

She believed.

Luna smiled and remarked, "Together, witches and fairies can get this done. Our combined magical powers can dispel the curse because we are strong together."

Luna asked the witches, "Please send your magical incantations to the sky now that the fairies will dance."

Suddenly, the witches began sending energy to the sky.

At that very moment, the other fairies began moving into a line, first a few, then slowly more. They gathered to form a grand dance to save their beloved forest from Rozsika's evil curse.

The fairies were determined to stop the awful spell. They moved together, organizing themselves in perfect harmony.

The fairies grasped hands. Their energies formed into magic circles. The fairies started chanting together. They could feel the strength of their magic increasing with each motion.

They said, "We embrace the wonder of our world!"

Nature's healing gave Luna energy. A wild wind sent off good vibrations of peace and rejuvenation, creating a symphony of nature that could be felt with every breath.

The sun and breeze combined to create balance, and everyone felt a newfound sense of strength.

Luna felt triumphant! Together the witches and fairies had succeeded!

Breaking the curse made everyone happy. The witches and fairies danced all night long. Everyone was delighted to see peace return to their forest.

The witches and fairies knew that their dance was a reminder that even in the darkest times, the light of hope and love would always shine.

www.ingramcontent.com/pod-product-compliance
Lightning Source LLC
Chambersburg PA
CBHW041912040426
42444CB00027BA/29